DEVOTIONS FOR COUPLES

INSPIRED LIVING SERIES

DEVOTIONS FOR COUPLES

BY

CECIL MURPHEY

New York Times Bestselling Author

eISBN: 978-1-937776-16-9
ISBN 13: 978-1-937776-87-9

OTHER BOOKS BY CECIL MURPHEY

Inspired Living Devotional Series:

Devotions for Couples
Devotions for Dieters
Devotions for Runners
Revitalize Your Prayer Life: Inspired
Living Series Companion

More Titles:

90 Minutes in Heaven (with Don Piper)
Gifted Hands: The Ben Carson
Story (with Dr. Ben Carson)
Rebel with a Cause (with Franklin Graham)
Because You Care: Spiritual Encouragement for
Caregivers (by Cecil Murphey and Twila Belk)
When Someone You Love No Longer Remembers
The Spirit of Christmas (by Cecil
Murphey and Marley Gibson)
Unleash the Writer Within
Knowing God, Knowing Myself
When a Man You Love Was Abused
When God Turned Off the Lights

A New Foreword

I wrote this book 30 years ago, and as I've read the pages again, I could change some sentences, but I wouldn't change a single statement or fact about love and marriage.

Even though my wife Shirley and I have had more than half a century together, there is one sentence I pray every morning. "Thank you, God, that Shirley and I have at least one more day together."

Those aren't empty words; I'm genuinely grateful for the days and the years we've already had. Shirley has had several serious illnesses. And she has a family history of cancer. A decade ago she had breast cancer and I thought I might lose her. She fully recovered, and the day after her surgery, is the day I began that simple prayer.

I know that one day we won't be together. But as long as both of us are alive, I want every day to be special. Not only do I thank God for Shirley each day, but our morning isn't complete without a long, passionate hug.

Over the years we've learned each other's ways so well that many times we know what the other wants or senses without a word between us.

I sometimes say that good marriages aren't built on a one-time falling in love, but in several cycles of love. Sexual attraction and sharing common goals are obvious first attractions. Later, many of us fall in love again because of the tenderness or faithfulness of our spouse. The older I become the more I value Shirley's companionship. She knows my flaws, accepts them, and still loves me.

Good marriages are built on deep passion that wanes, renews itself, and each time takes on a deeper meaning.

We don't love each other the same way we did when I was 22 years old, but this phase of our love relationship is certainly deeper. More than ever I realize how much of my life revolves around her and hers around mine.

And each day I'm thankful that God brought us together.

LOVING EACH OTHER

Love is patient and kind. Love is not jealous or boastful or proud. (1 Corinthians 13:4)

Week 1, Day 1

When Shirley and I were dating, her mother made a statement that went something like this: "Some married people are kinder to their friends than they are to each other." Over the years I've thought about those words often and determined it wouldn't apply to us.

Sometimes because we love each other, we tend to take the other for granted. We become more considerate of new relationships because we want to establish them. We already have a loving relationship with our lover and therefore do not show concern.

I've noticed that when many couples are in the dating stage, they're courteous and helpful. I've seen the dashing young fellow carefully open doors for the light of his life. I've often seen those same couples a year after their marriage. He gets out of the car and lets her get out by herself.

One of the things Shirley and I decided when we were dating was that I would continue opening doors for her all through our married life. I also said, "If I forget, I expect you to remind me." I'm still opening doors for Shirley because it's my way of saying I care about her and want to do little things for her.

True lovers constantly find ways to show they appreciate each other and to affirm the relationship they have.

True lovers enjoy each other. They do things together, whether it's working, participating in sports, or attending plays and concerts. They share common interests.

True lovers respect each other. They may disagree, but they allow for differences of opinion. When we really love another person, we don't pressure him or her to act contrary to his or her values.

We had a woman in our church who was very talented musically. She once said that people had appreciated her talent for years, but very few had appreciated her as a person. She needed affirmation as a human being and not just recognition of her abilities.

Lovers care by being sensitive to each other's hopes, fears, aspirations, dreams, and plans. The Apostle John writes, "Beloved, let us love one another." "Beloved" could be read as "dear friends," as it is in some translations. He's saying, "As friends, let's love one another." Lovers respect, love, and cherish each other, not only for today but throughout their lives.

Lord God, teach us the full dimensions of love as we discover more about each other and discover more about you. Amen.

AVAILABLE LOVE

… For God has said, "I will never fail you. I will never abandon you." (Hebrews 13:5)

Week 1, Day 2

I was involved in an automobile accident four years ago. A man in another car ran through a red light and hit me. My car was severely damaged, and I did not have another vehicle. Several friends told me how sorry they were about my situation. Many of them added something like "If there's anything we can do…." One friend, Bob, never made such a statement. He heard about the accident, called, and said, "For a few days we can get by with one car. We'd like to lend you our second car." Bob's love was available to me.

Often we want to spend time with our friends, but only at our convenience. There are times when we wish to be alone and resent the intrusion of other people and their problems. We like to choose our availability.

Yet true love is available at all times. That doesn't mean I always feel loving, or that I always feel good about being disturbed. But if I really love you I am available to you.

True lovers make themselves available to each other. Available to listen, to talk, to touch, to hold. Available lovers echo the words from Hebrews, "I will never forsake you."

We understand that promise because Jesus Christ gives us the perfect model. God says he will never leave us, and that he will never fail us in any way. True lovers work at imitating that ideal.

Faithful Lord, as we appreciate your availability, may we learn always to be available to each other. Amen.

But Why?

"The Lord did not set his heart on you and choose you because you were more numerous than other nations, for you were the smallest of all nations! Rather, it was simply that the Lord loves you, and he was keeping the oath he had sworn to your ancestors. (Deuteronomy 7:7–8a)

Week 1, Day 3

Shirley and I had dated nearly three months, and our relationship progressed nicely. We did things together. We talked. We prayed.

When did I start loving her? I have no idea. The consciousness of it came to me as I sat across a table from her during a Bible-study group. I had to leave early and didn't get to say good-bye. Just before I left, our eyes met, and we held that look. I knew then that I loved her. Somehow I knew from the expression in her eyes that she loved me, too.

Later I thought about it. I knew why I loved her. I could think of hundreds of reasons for loving her. But I just couldn't figure out why she loved me. A Christian as committed as Shirley could have had many others. But she had loved me. Why?

We've now been married a quarter of a century, and I still haven't answered the question. Just as well. It doesn't have an answer. It's enough to say, "She loves me."

I caught on to this through reading Deuteronomy 7 one evening. God prepared to take the Israelites into the new land, and he called them a holy people (that is, a people which he had separated for himself). He told them he had chosen them, but not because they were a great nation. In fact, he reminded them, "You were the fewest of all peoples." Then he told why he chose them: "It is because the Lord loves you."

If we can figure out a reason for God's love, we haven't truly understood love. We have no claims on him. We have no right. We don't deserve anything. Once we grasp that fact, we can appreciate the depth of his love.

God loves us, that's all we can say.

When we come right down to it, we can't really explain why we love each other any more than we can explain why God loves us. But then, does it really matter? Isn't it enough just to know?

Lord, thank you that _____ loves me. I don't understand why she/he loves me, any more than I understand why you love me. But I accept you both. Amen.

SENSITIVE LOVE

There was a man there named Zacchaeus. He was the chief tax collector in the region, and he had become very rich. He tried to get a look at Jesus, but he was too short to see over the crowd. So he ran ahead and climbed a sycamore-fig tree beside the road, for Jesus was going to pass that way. When Jesus came by, he looked up at Zacchaeus and called him by name. "Zacchaeus!" he said. "Quick, come down! I must be a guest in your home today." (Luke 19:2–5)

Week 1, Day 4

I've tried to visualize that scene. There was Zacchaeus, perhaps a foot shorter than the average person. Apparently he did not know Jesus. He climbed into a tree so he could see what Jesus looked like. Jesus passed along, looked up, saw that man. He called to him, "Come on down, Zacchaeus. I'm going to have lunch with you today." Of all the hundreds and thousands of people in that crowd, Jesus looked up and saw Zacchaeus. Jesus was sensitive to one man's needs.

That's how love works; it is sensitive to the needs and pain of other people.

Lovers understand each other intuitively. The closer they get, the more they realize there's a time to speak and there's also a time not to speak. They realize that on some occasions they need to sit in silence and hold hands. On occasion they need to walk out of the room and leave the other alone.

Sensitivity to others simply means that we are aware of where that person is. We care, and we reach out.

I can think of nothing worse than being filled with pain because of a problem and not being able to share it with anyone, to be present with a group of friends and yet not feel anyone is sensitive enough to ask or to care. True lovers don't read each other's minds, but they do read each other's moods. They may not know specifically when there is something wrong, but they sense that all is not right. One becomes sensitive to the other, takes the initiative, allowing the hurting one to respond and open the door.

Jesus saw Zacchaeus' need and took the first step. Zacchaeus said "yes" by coming down from the tree. In the same way, lovers are sensitive to each other, always caring and always wanting to heal each others' pains.

Lord God, teach us to be sensitive to each other's needs and moods. Amen.

LOVE AND FEELINGS

A second is equally important: 'Love your neighbor as your-self.' (Matthew 22:39)

Week 1, Day 5

My late friend Charlie Shedd shared an incident from the early days of his marriage. One day he found a note from his wife. It read, "Dear Charlie, I hate you. Love, Martha."

The note sounds contradictory, with both hate and love in the same sentence. Perhaps Martha's choice of hate implied more anger than she really felt. But that message also says to me that we can love people and still feel angry or irritated.

One of the problems we have with love is that we think of it as purely an emotion. In reality, true love is not an emotion. We may have feelings related to love. In literature and music we're always talking about feelings of love, falling in love; but when our love depends upon feelings, we become fickle lovers. Actually, love is commitment. I often define love as caring in action.

If I really love a person I'm going to do what I feel is best for that individual. It will not depend on whether or not I feel good about it; I do it because it's the right thing to do.

I love Shirley. I think our marriage is a good marriage. Some days I don't "feel" loving toward her. Some days I don't even think about how I feel about her. But I am committed to her. She is the most important person in my life. If our relationship depended purely upon my feelings, it would be like a yo-yo. Some days I would love her, and on other days I might not. It would depend upon how I felt at the moment. It also might depend upon how I felt about myself. Some days I'm not physically or emotionally on top, and my feelings reflect that.

When Jesus said that the second greatest commandment was to love your neighbor as yourself, he was not talking about feelings. He was talking about action.

When I said to Shirley for the first time, "I love you," my words were based on several things. I had strong feelings of physical attraction. More than that, I knew I was making a commitment to her. She had become important to my life. I was also saying that I wanted to be with her and I wanted our lives intertwined. I was convinced that God had brought us together. Because he had brought us together, I knew that I would care about her even on those days when I might feel emotionally down.

God, thank you for our love, which includes feelings. Yet our love transcends emotions. Thank you that we are committed to each other because we are committed to you. Amen.

LISTENING LOVERS

Answer me when I call to you, O God who declares me innocent. Free me from my troubles. Have mercy on me and hear my prayer. You can be sure of this: The Lord set apart the godly for himself. The Lord will answer when I call to him. (Psalm 4:1–3)

Week 1, Day 6

Gene and Liz divorced after twenty-three years of marriage. Fortunately they have a happy ending to their story—they remarried two years later.

"We had stopped talking. We took each other for granted. We bored each other. Our separation and divorce made us rethink why we had married in the first place," Gene told me.

"We learned to listen and to talk to each other," Liz said as they held hands.

Lovers listen to each other. They concentrate on the words and even understand more than the words themselves say. If we're truly listening lovers, we feel what the other feels and want joy or pain to be a mutual experience.

I know that's true because of the relationship that Shirley and I have shared. Even more, we base this on a greater fact than our own relationship. We base it on our relationship with the Lover. Throughout the Bible, all the praying men and women knew that God heard them. Psalm 4 is only one of the hundreds of examples of the godly stating that God hears when they talk.

It's when we talk, and know we're heard, that our relationship becomes more solid.

Great Lover, teach me to listen to _____ *in the same way that I know you hear and understand me. Amen.*

FRIENDS AND LOVERS

Love is patient and kind. Love is not jealous or boastful or proud. (1 Corinthians 13:4)

Week 1, Day 7

Last week I had lunch with Kiki, a writer friend. A few days after that I took my secretary to lunch. Shirley occasionally goes to lunch with Marvin or Barry—people she works with.

For Shirley and me this creates no problem. Those people are either co-workers or friends or both. I have several people I feel especially close to—and some of them are female.

We feel our attitude reflects a biblical view. Paul, the apostle, writes about one of the qualities of love in 1 Corinthians. He says that love is not jealous. That means love allows freedom. Love gives lovers the opportunity to enjoy the companionship and friendship with members of the opposite sex.

We overcome jealousy by offering each other assurance of our affection and commitment. I know Shirley loves me; Shirley knows I love her. We have a good relationship built on trust and our own friendship for each other. Beyond trust, I also want Shirley to grow as a person. True love allows the other to move in several directions. I want her to develop relationships with other people. She allows me the same freedom.

Jealousy, on the other hand, springs from insecurity. Jealousy means there is doubt. It may be doubt on a man's part of his love for his wife. Jealousy may mean doubt on her part that he is being faithful. Jealousy arises from uncertainty and asks questions such as, "How could he possibly love me?" True Christian love removes jealousy. Mutual commitment gives us a sense of well-being and the realization that we are loved by the person most important to us. We are not the other's total world. I love Shirley, she is the most important person in my world, but she is not the only person. Nor would I wish to be the only person in her world.

We accept and encourage other friendships for each other. Because we are secure in our relationship, our love continues to deepen. We are both free—free to allow the other to have a wide range of friends. We are free to be open to other people.

Great God, thank you that you've given us the capacity to love many people. I thank you for my lover, and for my friends. Amen.

Praying Lovers

I waited patiently for the Lord to help me, and he turned to me and heard my cry. (Psalm 40:1)

Week 2, Day 1

I was twenty-one and engaged to a girl. My mind told me I was the luckiest man in the world. She was attractive, bright, loyal—the adjectives went on and on. Just one problem. Deep inside me, a voice said, "She is not for you."

We had met while I was in the process of discovering the Christian faith for myself. I knew that following Jesus Christ meant letting go of her. Eventually we broke up.

I remember praying, "Lord, I don't know how to pick out a wife. If you want me to marry, you send her to me."

A few weeks later I met Shirley at church. I knew that night that God had sent her into my life; I knew God had chosen her for me.

How did I know? Call it a deep inner assurance. Call it God's silent voice. Mostly I call it answered prayer—and not only answered to me, but to Shirley also.

As I later learned, she had been dating a man for six months and while everyone told her he was a good catch, in her heart Shirley knew it would not work. She broke off with him.

Then we met. But before our meeting, both of us had asked the Lord for the right person to come into our lives.

After the service, we introduced ourselves, talked, and went out for coffee. I said, "Shirley, I think God sent you into my life." After explaining, I added, "If you're not open to exploring a relationship with me, you'd better back out now."

She smiled and said, "I'm open."

I knew I didn't love her then. I also knew that if God brought us together in answer to our individual prayers, love would emerge.

It did. We married six months later. But between our first date and our marriage vows, we learned a lot about each other. We spent six nights a week on dates, mostly involved in church activities. We learned each other's moods, interests, and short-comings. We also prayed together each evening. While we talked to God about many things, right from the first time we both said, "God, if your plans include us together, then guide us. If not, show us both."

The Lord answered those prayers. We have since established a daily routine of praying together.

Through the years we have grown together and we believe our praying together has been a major factor.

Just the other morning when Shirley and I had our devotional time together she prayed, "Lord, thank you for our love, which continues to grow stronger each year."

Lord, you have a right person for me. Help both of us to know. Amen.

PRAYING FOR OUR LOVERS

So we keep on praying for you, asking our God to enable you to live a life worthy of his call. May he give you the power to accomplish all the good things your faith prompts you to do. (2 Thessalonians 1:11)

Week 2, Day 2

Each day I pray for Shirley. I don't pray for her only out of habit. I talk to God about her because of my love for Shirley. I want Shirley to be the very best Christian that she can be. I recognize talents in her which God has given, and I want them perfected. I recognize weaknesses in her that I want to see corrected.

I think that is the intent of Paul's words when he wrote that he prayed for the Thessalonians. He prayed for them to be worthy of the Christian life, to be filled with God's power, to be perfect in the work of faith.

Lovers also pray like that. When we love someone, we want that person to be as perfect as possible. We care about every area of the other's life. I think Shirley is a better person today than she was when we first met. She's more in touch with herself, more in harmony with Jesus Christ. Part of her growth has come about because I have supported her in all kinds of ways, but especially through prayer.

Lovers pray for each other because they are important to each other.

Shirley and I both realized early in our relationship that we made a wholesome trio—God, Shirley, and me. We learned that we could talk to each other, and then we could talk to God about each other. Often we pray for God to increase our love and our understanding. We pray for patience. We learn to take our problems to God together. Prayer has been a very exciting and special part of our life together.

Holy God, thank you that you hear our prayers as we pray for each other and as we grow in unity. Amen.

THE BIG TEMPTATION

Run from sexual sin! No other sin so clearly affects the body as this one does. For sexual immorality is a sin against your own body. Don't you realize that your body is the temple of the Holy Spirit, who lives in you and was given to you by God? You do not belong to yourself. (1 Corinthians 6:18–19)

Week 2, Day 3

You love each other. You're thinking of marriage, the future, possibly children—all the kinds of dreams that lovers have. You spend a lot of time together, just being close, kissing, holding and enjoying each other.

And somewhere in that relationship comes the big temptation. It happens to all lovers.

"But everyone else has sex before marriage," I've heard some say.

"We're going to get married anyway."

"How can something so beautiful as this be wrong?"

Sex is wonderful—God created it. He also reserves it for special people—married couples. It's worth waiting for.

Even more significant, sex before marriage means selling out. It's a giving in to temptation and disobeying God. Paul's words ring clear: "Avoid immorality." Don't yield to temptation.

Lovers, in the passion of the moment, fail to realize what sex was intended for. It was to be the full joining together of one man and one woman. The Old Testament says that Adam "knew" his wife. I like that word. Sex, as intended by God, is the ultimate self-giving and self-receiving in relationships.

Not long ago I talked with a group of singles. One of them, who made no secret of her frequent sexual encounters, told me she gave in because she needed to be loved.

Before I had a chance to respond, another member of the group said, "There are other ways to be loved."

A second person spoke up, "You sold yourself too cheaply."

I agreed with both, especially the second. God intended for that special relationship after couples say "I do." It's the fulfillment of a relationship.

The Apostle Paul brings this out when he uses marriage as an analogy of Christ and the church. A husband gives himself to his wife and she to him. But their purpose, beyond the enjoyment of the sexual act, is crowned in the unity they create. "The two shall become one," say Genesis and Paul.

Lovers are always on a journey together, always finding new meaning to their relationship. Sex, which God intended to begin after marriage, is the door that leads into deeper relationships; and it happens without guilt or shame or fear.

If you're tempted, and most lovers are, you don't have to give in. If you've already given in, don't yield again. As Christian lovers, you have the strength of Jesus Christ, your greatest resource.

Lord Jesus, remind us that sex is reserved for marriage and may we have the strength to wait until then to experience it. Amen.

WITHOUT RESENTMENT

Love is patient and kind. Love is not jealous or boastful or proud. (1 Corinthians 13:4)

Week 2, Day 4

Some years ago I read a novel, its title and author forgotten, about a woman who married a man she loved. He did not love her, although he was fond of her. For thirty years she would not allow anyone to speak against him, even when he deserved it. She bore patiently with his foul temper, as well as the thoughtless ways he acted, all because she loved him.

Near the end of the book, he died; but he confessed that her love had finally won him. He had learned to love her without realizing it. Why? Because she never resented him or wavered in her faithfulness. She loved him.

I can think of no greater quality of love than that which refuses to resent and would not consider retaliating.

Often when a person speaks against us, or says anything unkind, we find ourselves becoming angry. We also think of getting even. "I'll do the same thing to him that he did to me." "She gossiped about me, so…"

Real love pushes such thoughts aside. Love is commitment to a cause, a person, or a faith. That love doesn't waver simply because things go wrong.

Mature love knows how to overlook failures. It can close its ears against angry words. It has no desire to get even.

In the novel mentioned above, the woman said to her husband on the night of their marriage, "I love you enough for both of us." Her constancy throughout the book proved the reality of that love.

Reflecting on that novel reminds me of God's love toward me. No one needs to remind me of my failures, my lack of devotion, or my straying from God. Yet one thing always brings me back—his constant love which always welcomes me without recrimination.

A few years ago I saw this illustrated in Jesus' parable of the prodigal son in Luke 15. The younger son went astray but eventually came to himself. He decided to return home, not as a son, but as a laborer in the fields. Before he had a chance to speak, the father was standing in the road, arms outstretched. He didn't lecture and he didn't resent. He said, "My son who was lost is now found."

The father rejoiced over the loved one's return. He didn't remind the young man of wasted funds and riotous living. He simply loved the son—as he had all along.

That's not always easy. When we feel betrayed, rejected, slighted, or taken advantage of, we want to retaliate. Or at least resentment builds up. When it happens twice or three times, or perhaps half a dozen times, the volcano erupts. Anger spews out. That's the natural way for many of us.

Yet the Apostle Paul reminds us that true love doesn't work that way. We learn from God that love keeps on giving of itself. It overlooks the occasions for resentment. It stores up no grievances. It only gives of itself.

My Lord and Teacher, take away resentment. Replace it with the love that suffers long and harbors no ill feelings. Amen.

NEEDY LOVE

Jacob's well was there; and Jesus, tired from the long walk, sat wearily beside the well about noontime. (John 4:6)

Week 2, Day 5

When I dated Shirley, I began realizing that I needed her. She supplied qualities I didn't have. She balanced my life. I was the spontaneous, quickly decisive, easily involved type. Shirley preferred to look a situation over thoroughly, think about it a few days, and then make a decision. She slowed me down. And in those occasional moments when life tumbled in on me and I doubted myself, she was always there to reassure me.

Lovers, no matter how strong their personalities, always need other people. When we love another, we instinctively (and usually unconsciously) select a person who possesses the qualities we lack. We need that other to be whole.

God never created any of us to be self-sufficient. God made us with weaknesses and strengths so that we could learn interdependence. A common need becomes the basis for human relationships.

Only recently I saw Jesus as a needy person. In the story found in John 4, he had been with his disciples, and he was physically tired. He sat down by the well, and they went into the city for food.

It struck me as I read that passage: Jesus had a need. For him, it was to rest his physical body, but it was a need nonetheless. And an outcast woman came by at just the time Jesus rested. She had a need—to hear the good news.

That's often how God works. In this case, a tired Jesus, needing rest, sat at the place where the guilt-laden woman came. He found rest; she found peace. Both had their needs met.

One of the great things about lovers is that they meet each other's needs—and often without being aware of it. They do it instinctively, because they care. And caring enables us to meet the needs of the other person.

Great Lord of life, help us accept our needs, and may we open ourselves so that both you and our lover may meet those needs. Amen.

PROTECTING LOVE

Most important of all, continue to show deep love for each other, for love covers a multitude of sins. (1 Peter 4:8)

Week 2, Day 6

When reading the Old Testament, I used to marvel at the way God talked about Israel and to Israel. When he talked to them, he scathingly pointed out their failures and meted out punishment. Yet when God talked about Israel, it was always as his special people. If they had failures, outsiders would not know it. It was a family matter.

Love protects its own. It doesn't protect by denying shortcomings and failures. Love knows reality, but it doesn't nag. Mature lovers find ways of sheltering the other from criticism and rejection.

Wayne told me that after he had been married four years, he had an affair. One night he was out with the other woman, a car hit them head-on, and the woman died hours later in the hospital.

The incident happened in a moderate-sized town where Wayne held a responsible position. He called his wife, Janet, from the hospital, blurted out the story, and hung up before she could reply. He expected that when he eventually went home, Janet would be gone.

Instead she rushed to the hospital and sat in the waiting room with him.

After the other woman's death and as the story circulated, Janet never criticized Wayne. From her lips, no one knew it had been an extramarital affair. By her constant presence at his side, no tongues wagged. Janet's love was strong enough to stand by her husband and protect him.

Because of Janet's consistent love, she was able to get him to attend church with her, and eventually both of them committed themselves to Christ.

That's the protecting love true lovers understand. They know that their love can overcome all obstacles. They remain steadfast in the midst of trials and even rejections. The covering of sins may not be this extreme. It doesn't matter what the failure; true love protects its own from criticism.

Lord, may our love be so strong that it will cover any weakness or failure in the other because we understand your love that covers all our sins. Amen.

POSSESSIVE LOVE

[Love] … does not demand its own way. It is not irritable, and it keeps no record of being wronged. (1 Corinthians 13:5)

Week 2, Day 7

During my college days, several of us were talking about marriage. There were two fellows in the group who were not yet married. One of them asked us, "What do you like about your wife?"

I don't remember all the answers we gave, but I remember one person said, "She makes me feel like the most important person in the world, and she's always there to encourage me."

That's mature love, not a possessive love. That man's wife didn't stay with him so he could make her a better person, though I think he did that. One of the qualities of true love is that it affirms the other rather than attempting to possess or control. Real love liberates; real love gives freedom to be ourselves. Frederick Perls wrote, "You did not come into this world to live up to my expectations. And I did not come into the world to live up to yours."

Healthy love means I want what's best for you. I want to offer what you need from me in a way that preserves your freedom, allows you to have your own feelings, think your own thoughts, and make your own decisions.

Yet some lovers are often more possessive than they realize. Here are some questions to ask ourselves: (1) Is it more important to me that you be pleased with yourself or that I be pleased with you? (2) Is it more important that you attain the goals you have set for yourself, or that you attain the goals I want for you? (3) Does my love enable you to relate more successfully to other people? (4) Do I rejoice when you are liked and appreciated by other people, or do I want you to always make me the center of your world?

Three years ago my willingness to liberate came to the test. Shirley talked of going back to college. If she went, it meant I would see less of her, as she would be involved in her studies and have less time for me. It also meant that she would be doing less work around the house and I would have to take on a greater share of the responsibilities. I'm glad that without hesitation I could say, "Go back to school if that's what you want." That experience helped me realize I wanted her to be happy and to expand her world.

That's how true lovers relate. They always want the best for the other, without holding back and without trying to possess.

My Master and my God, help our love to be freeing, and may we encourage each other to expand to our full capacity. Amen.

Rejoicing Love

[Love] does not rejoice about injustice but rejoices whenever the truth wins out. (1 Corinthians 13:6)

Week 3, Day 1

Within a year our writers' group became a tightly knit fellowship of eight people. We all wanted to write, publish, and find fulfillment through print.

As it turned out, I was the first in the group to have an article accepted, and later the first to have a book accepted for publication. I remember the night I shared the news with the others.

One of the members said all the right words of congratulations and even smiled. But I knew him well enough to know that he was not fully rejoicing with me. I shrugged it off. He was having problems with his marriage, and his job had turned out to be tedious.

A few weeks later, I told the group that two articles I had written had both come back, rejected. This same fellow said, "Sorry," but his eyes told me he didn't grieve for me.

In the next few weeks, I realized that he had conflicting emotions going on inside him. On the one hand, he was my friend and wanted me to succeed. But when I did, he found himself jealous. It made him feel inadequate because he had been writing as long as I had and had sold nothing.

By contrast, when I had my second book published, Suzanne heard about it and called me. "I was so excited when I heard your good news, almost as though I had had a book accepted myself!" I believed her words and knew that she spoke the truth.

Her words lived out the statement that Saint Paul makes in his famous love chapter that love "does not rejoice at wrong, but rejoices in the right." Suzanne didn't get happy over failures and rejections, but rejoiced over success in my life.

True lovers want each other's success. They're not competitors, even if both share the same occupation or have similar goals in life. True lovers can rejoice when the other gets a break, wins recognition, or advances at work. True lovers genuinely feel sad when the other has any setback. True lovers encourage, wanting only the best for each other.

I saw this clearly with one couple who had a new baby. The wife, not the homemaker type, had executive ability and held down a good job. Three months after the baby's birth she returned to work. Her husband, a teacher, became a househusband until the child entered school. He was willing to let his own career slide into the background so his wife could advance herself. The husband was often teased about his choice. When he joined the work force again, he had trouble explaining to prospective employers why he had not worked for six years.

Was it worth it for the couple? They both said, "We're happy. We would do it all over again if the situation arose."

While that's an unusual incident, it illustrates rejoicing love, which is happy when the other has a chance at advancement or success, and is willing to let personal desires move into the background.

Lovers find happiness with each other, they are happy because they make each other happy.

God, you've enabled us to rejoice in each other's love. Increase our happiness with each other as we grow in our relationship with you. Amen.

INITIATING LOVE

We love each other because he loved us first. (1 John 4:19)

Week 3, Day 2

I remember the first time Grace and Ed came to my office. They discussed all the things wrong in their marriage; yet both of them admitted that they loved each other. I looked at Ed and said, "Do you ever tell Grace that you love her?"

He said, "I used to, but I just got tired of always taking the initiative."

The shock on Grace's face showed me that she didn't realize he had felt that way. As we talked further, it came out that for their first three or four years of marriage they talked of their love and expressed it. Ed said, "Our good times came about because I took the first steps. Finally I got tired. I was doing all the loving, and she was doing all the receiving. She only gave if I gave first." She defended herself and said, "I was always available to you."

Ed said, "Available, yes. But you never once said, 'I love you' unless I said it first."

Grace finally admitted that was so, but she had not realized it. She had concentrated so much on her needs to be loved, to be appreciated, to be affirmed, and to be accepted that it had not occurred to her to take the first steps in lovemaking, talking, or even holding hands.

Some people take initiative much easier than others; some people are followers. True love is both giving and receiving. We have an example of giving: God. God loved and God gave.

I went through a very difficult time during my days as a teacher. I came home one day, and Shirley could tell by the worried look on my face that everything wasn't right. She asked me what had happened.

"Just a heavy day," I mumbled.

Shirley put her arm around me. She kissed my cheek, but said nothing. Then I pulled her close and we stood in the living room, embracing for a long time. When I released her, I said, "I needed you to hold me like that."

Shirley grabbed me again and held tight. In those quiet moments together, the problems at school didn't seem as overwhelming as they had when I came home.

True lovers not only learn to interpret each other's words and gestures, but they take the initiative. They don't wait for the other to express a need. Their sensitivity to moods and needs impels them to say, "Here, let me help." They also learn to say the words that the other needs to hear.

Our Father and our God , you took the initiative in loving us. Free us to initiate conversation, to touch, to love, or to do whatever the other needs. Amen.

LOVERS' HANDS

A man with leprosy came and knelt in front of Jesus, begging to be healed. "If you are willing, you can heal me and make me clean," he said. Moved with compassion, Jesus reached out and touched him. "I am willing," he said. "Be healed!" (Mark 1:40–41)

Week 3, Day 3

I'm a toucher. That's part of my nature. I express a lot of my feelings with my hands. Some people I hug, with others I shake hands. Sometimes I touch a shoulder, hold a hand, or kiss a cheek. Not that I plan how I'm going to react, because most of the time it's spontaneous.

Part of the way my hands talk is to show that I'm listening. Sometimes I sit next to the hospital bed and hold a man's hand. By that physical contact I am, as much as possible, sharing in his pain.

Touching can create intimacy. When I touch Shirley and she allows it, there is a commitment established. When I put my arm around Shirley, one of the things my actions say is, "I'm here, actually present with you. My mind is not on tomorrow's problems or today's left-over business."

Lovers listen with their hands. A gentle stroking or a warm touch opens up the other and says, "It's all right for you to be free with me. I'm here and I'm listening."

When I hold Shirley's hand and she's talking, I respond unconsciously by the pressure of my fingers. When she's not feeling her best, she may put her head on my shoulder, and I stroke her hair. My fingers say, "It's all right, Honey." I'm offering comfort while listening.

Lovers' hands communicate when there are no words to be said. They sometimes speak even stronger than words.

When I think of lovers' hands I remember many incidents in the life of Jesus. He healed, but even more significant he touched physical bodies, even vile ones. He touched a leper, a sick woman, a blind man. The hand of the original Lover communicated God's love.

Lord God, as my lover and I touch each other and express our love, may it also symbolize our mutual love for you. Amen.

LOVERS' EYES

The eyes of the Lord watch over those who do right; his ears are open to their cries for help. (Psalm 34:15)

Week 3, Day 4

Trish and Chuck sat in the booth across from me at lunch. During the hour we stayed, their eyes kept focusing on each other. Little verbal communication took place between them. They had told me before that they were "just friends."

Their eyes told me differently. They stared like two lovers who see nothing else in the world. Even when I talked, their eyes moved from my face to each other, quite unconsciously and with no intention of being rude. They did not even know what they were doing.

Lovers' eyes do that. I've been aware, for instance, that sometimes at a party Shirley and I will be across the room from each other. Our eyes meet and something flashes between us. This love signal is a lover's way of saying, "You're wonderful and I love you."

I'm not giving lessons about eye contact or how to let your eyes speak. It's an unconscious part of the chemistry of being in love. The eyes hold each other's gaze a little too long. They find themselves searching past faces and bodies at a party or at church, looking for the loved one. Lovers feel the need to gaze constantly at each other. I suspect the eye contact is a nonverbal way of saying, "I love you."

Lovers' eyes also appear in the Bible, because God, the original Lover, looks at us constantly. In several places it says that the eyes of the Lord are upon the righteous. Not that God literally has eyes, but it's a figure of speech to help us know that God "sees" everything, and especially to remind us that he takes care of and protects his beloved children.

That's how lovers' eyes work—they constantly shift to the object of their love, shutting out everything else.

Do this the next time you see two people's eyes trained on each other. Notice how beautiful they are. Why not? They're alive, alert. They glow from an inward source. They communicate with the other in ways that don't need words. The eyes have a love language all their own.

Lord, as I gaze into _____'s eyes and see love, may it remind me that your love is even greater. Amen.

WHEN LOVERS FIGHT

What is causing the quarrels and fights among you? Don't they come from the evil desires at war within you? (James 4:1)

Week 3, Day 5

"All couples fight." I've been hearing that dictum stated for at least the last fifteen years. Counselors and advisors on marriage scoff at couples who say they never fight. They assume that couples who never fight don't show their true feelings to each other.

But who says it has to be that way?

Shirley and I do not fight, and we have never fought. We have had disagreements, but we've always been able to handle them without any serious difficulty. I'm impulsive and sometimes irritation creeps in because Shirley does not respond as quickly as I do. There have been occasions when I have moved too fast for her and have caused irritation to arise in my wife. We have been able to tell each other then and there. To us this does not constitute fighting. For some, it may.

Fighting, as I understand it, implies that couples speak angry words and then respond to them either verbally or nonverbally. It implies serious differences and disagreements. It also implies that at least one of them has lost his or her temper. I'm not convinced that this must be normal in the Christian experience.

Why do we have to fight? One reason people fight is that they store up hurts. When enough pain accumulates, the fire of anger erupts. One good way to avoid a fight is to face a conflict as soon as it appears.

Over the years I've hurt Shirley and she's hurt me. Both of us have done it unintentionally. Sometimes it happens by saying a thoughtless word, or teasing in a way that the other misunderstands. We have tried, as soon as there is an opportunity, to say to the other, "I am hurt." That clears the air.

To me the strongest incentive for not fighting is acknowledging that we are one in Jesus Christ. He enables us to live in harmony.

The book of James talks about warring among Christians in a church. Fighting goes on, the author says, because people have evil desires. Each wants his/her own way. By going in different directions, they conflict.

Yet we know that when lovers seek the same goals and attempt to make Jesus Christ the center of life, fighting stops.

Lord God, teach us to live in harmony with each other as we try to make you always the center of our lives. Amen.

FIGHTING FAIR

Get rid of all bitterness, rage, anger, harsh words, and slander, as well as all types of evil behavior. Instead, be kind to each other, tenderhearted, forgiving one another, just as God through Christ has forgiven you. (Ephesians 4:31–32)

Week 3, Day 6

"Jo and I like to fight because making up is such fun," Hal jokingly said. Perhaps the making up is fun.

But I'm convinced that in the ideal relationship we work toward living together in harmony. It is because of our weakness as human beings that we fight. If we fight, there are some good ways to handle it. We might ask ourselves these questions:

Do I know what we're differing about? Sometimes couples haven't really listened to each other. They may be saying two different things or dealing with different problems. She may be talking about money, and he may be yelling about time. When strong differences arise, it's important that both understand exactly where they're differing.

Do I understand the other's position? Sometimes people do differ, including lovers. One way to bring peace is to ask myself, "Do I understand how he/she feels about this?" It's important to know what the other thinks before we argue too strongly. We may need to ask ourselves, "Can I get outside of myself a little and understand my lover's position?" That helps put things in perspective.

Are we hurting each other? Often the argument is not the important thing. It's really a dumping ground for stored-up anger, for guilt and unresolved difficulties that have finally surfaced.

Why did I get hurt? We all have touchy areas in our lives. Some things bother us that may not bother other people. For instance, I may joke about my big nose, but it hurts me if you joke about it, because it's a sensitive area with me. Shirley may comment that she speaks slowly, but if I make a remark about it, I can be offensive.

Am I sensitive to my lover's moods? I am at my best in the daytime. By night my internal clock is usually running down. I've noticed that when I'm very tired, it's difficult to talk to me about a serious item. Sometimes at the end of a day when Shirley is still revved up, she will suggest that we do something or go somewhere. At that moment I'm tired and it shows on my face. She's learned to read me. She's learned to know when not to talk to me about important decisions.

In the same way, there are times when I know that Shirley is not ready to talk about an item. I postpone it until she is ready. Lovers learn to do that. It's not that they're hiding or denying anything, but we're sensitive to each other's moods and temperament and wait until the other is ready to discuss an important subject.

Can I forgive? When people disagree, we need to learn to say, "I'm sorry." Saint Paul exhorts the Christians at Ephesus to be tenderhearted toward each other, to forgive. And he uses a marvelous example. He says we must forgive one another in the same way Christ has forgiven us. He makes his meaning clear: Because Christ forgives us, lovers have an obligation to forgive each other.

Forgiving God, in those times when we disagree or even fight, help us to come to peaceful terms and to forgive each other as you have forgiven us. Amen.

Saying Loving Words

"I have loved you, my people with an everlasting love. With unfailing love I have drawn you to myself. (Jeremiah 31:3)

Week 3, Day 7

When couples come to me for counseling, one of the things I urge them to do is to keep love alive. And one way to keep love alive is to express it frequently to each other. There are all kinds of physical gestures to communicate our love, such as touching with our hands or the way we look at each other. But we can't ever beat simply saying, "I love you."

Men tend to stop saying those three words after they're married. Perhaps it has to do without our macho image, or the belief that men aren't supposed to be as free to express feelings as women. Regardless of the reasons, it doesn't mean that there is no need to say the words. Couples need to keep speaking the familiar words "I love you."

I can think of nothing sadder than to love and not say those words. My father loved me. I'm sure of that. He died when he was eighty-four. But in all those years, from the day I was born until the day he died, he never said, "I love you," not to me nor to any of my brothers and sisters. It was not that my father did not love; he simply could not say, "I love you." It would have meant so much to us if he could have said those three special words.

We also need to hear words from God himself of his love for us. Although God says it in hundreds of places and in dozens of different ways, nowhere does he say it more clearly than in Jeremiah 31:3. He assures us not only that he loves us, but that his love never ends.

True lovers want that kind of love toward each other, a love that goes on and on and never stops. And because it goes on and on, they keep expressing it.

Sometimes the words sound as though they come by rote. I would still rather hear them spoken that way than not to hear them at all. I need assurance of being loved. I suspect we all do. And as we say and hear the three words, our love continues to grow.

God of heaven, we love you and we love each other. Help us always to remember to say "I love you" to you and to each other. Amen.

PRIVATE SPACES

Before daybreak the next morning, Jesus got up and went out to an isolated place to pray. (Mark 1:35)

Week 4, Day 1

I learned a lot about private spaces from Shirley. One time, only weeks before our marriage, I wanted her to go somewhere with me. "I just need to be alone," she said.

In the months that followed (and the years since), the importance of private spaces has become clear to me. We need times to separate ourselves, even from the people we love the most. We need moments when we can reflect and integrate what's happening to us.

True love, I learned, makes allowances for private spaces. I've also learned to make private spaces for myself. I do it mostly with running. I go off alone for forty minutes to an hour, usually by myself, and don't want to talk to anyone.

We all need private spaces; some need those spaces more than others. Shirley needs it more than I do, because by nature she's more private. She makes many important decisions in solitude. I like to talk with friends I trust, hear what they say, and then if I'm still not sure, in privacy I decide.

We're all different. True lovers not only understand the difference in the other, but encourage it as well.

In the New Testament, Jesus gave a prime example of private spaces. It says in Mark's Gospel that long before day, he went to a private place and prayed. Afterwards the disciples brought sick people to him and he healed them. He preached everywhere. But first he sought a private space.

Lovers need that private space away from each other and all the crowding noises of the day. We need the opportunity to reflect and to make decisions. In those times of solitude we grow.

Lord of life, help us encourage each other's private spaces as we mutually seek to follow you. Amen.

EVERYTHING KNOWN

Now we see things imperfectly, like puzzling reflections in a mirror, but then we will see everything with perfect clarity... then I will know everything completely, just as God now knows me completely. (1 Corinthians 13:12)

Week 4, Day 2

Two starry-eyed lovers sit on the sofa before me. We're planning their marriage ceremony. They hold hands and let their eyes roam over each other's bodies as only true lovers do.

I've been asking them about communicating with each other. "Oh, no problem there," she answers quickly. "We can talk about everything. Just everything in the world."

"That's right," he adds. "We're absolutely free. We know everything about each other."

But no one knows everything about anyone else. We've all hidden more below the surface than we realize. All of us have deep feelings that we're not aware of. It's not that lovers consciously hide information from each other. But during the dating period, everything doesn't surface. If it did, both parties would suffocate from information pollution.

The other person is always a mystery. She may enjoy having people around and suddenly want privacy. He may be moody in the morning, yet alert at night. She may keep the house looking neat, but opening the cupboards and drawers reveals disaster projects. He may leave tops off toothpaste and never refill the roll of toilet paper. Lovers never know those facts until they live together. Those are areas they discover together.

Sometimes our feelings run too deep to put into words. When my father died, Shirley had trouble expressing her grief. I'm more verbal, and it's easier for me to ventilate my feelings. When Dad died, I talked about my loss, wept a little, and experienced an increase in energy. Shirley said little about his death, and I never saw her cry. Months later she finally talked about her sense of loss and the depth of her relationship with my father—deeper than I had suspected. I learned something new about my wife through that episode of our lives.

I realize Shirley will never know everything about me, but I realize, too, that only one person truly knows and fully understands me: Jesus Christ. I've pledged my life not only to seek him (that's my first priority), but also to spend my life knowing and loving Shirley better.

Lord of life, I love _____ *and while I'll never know him/her perfectly, help me make knowing him/her a determined search until that day we're both made perfect in Jesus Christ. Amen.*

TRANSPARENT LOVERS

When Simon Peter realized what had happened, he fell to his knees before Jesus and said, "Oh, Lord, please leave me—I'm too much of a sinner to be around you." (Luke 5:8)

Week 4, Day 3

One of the beauties of lovers is that they learn to be transparent with each other. Many times we don't know how we feel or what we think about a person, an issue, a project until we actually say the words.

Here's the way I like to say it: "We know about ourselves only what we reveal about ourselves."

Lovers, because they are intimate and caring for each other, can open themselves to transparency. True lovers are always seeking to be more open to each other and, whether they recognize this or not, to know themselves better.

Opening myself to Shirley is rather easy. I trust her. I know she has my interests at heart. I can say things to her that I can say to no one else. It works the same way with Shirley. She is a much more private person than I am and does not speak about her feelings as easily as I do. I know that when she expresses deep emotions, she does this because she trusts me and is making herself vulnerable to me.

Some lovers can't handle transparency. They run from it or divert it. They have learned all kinds of methods of doing that. Sometimes they interrupt a statement. Other times they tell a funny story to relieve the tension or to break the mood. On other occasions they interrupt nonverbally. They let their eyes wander or they start doing something with their bodies, such as tapping their foot or their fingers. They might pick up a paper and start reading.

The New Testament tells how Peter learned about himself. He and his friends had fished all night and caught nothing. Jesus came along the next morning and told them to put their nets over the side. Peter scoffed at that and said, "Hey, we worked all night and didn't get a thing." His statement implied, "We're fishermen; we ought to know." Finally Peter said, "But because you give us the word, we'll do it." They put their nets over and pulled out a heavy load of fish. Peter turned to Jesus and said, "Depart from me Lord. I'm a sinful man."

The point of this story is that Peter realized his sinfulness when he came face to face with Jesus Christ. If someone had said to Peter, "You're a sinner," he might not have acknowledged it. But he said the words with his own lips. That's part of transparency.

We speak the words that come from our hearts, and as we speak them we hear ourselves and learn about ourselves.

Lord God, teach me to be open to my love and even more open to you, that I might learn more about myself. Amen.

Wearing Masks

[Jesus said,] "When you pray, don't be like the hypocrites who love to pray publicly on street corners and in the synagogues where everyone can see them. I tell you the truth, that is all the reward they will ever get." (Matthew 6:5)

Week 4, Day 4

Jesus gave a lesson on prayer. He said, "Don't be like the hypocrites." At certain hours of prayer, those religious folks just "happened to find themselves" in a public place. There they practiced their praying so that others would see them. Jesus said that if we really want to pray, we should go to a private place where only God sees us, and then God will reward us for our prayers.

He used the word "hypocrite," which literally means "a play actor." In the early days of drama, actors held masks over their faces, so the audience would be aware of the emotion the actor was trying to portray.

Most of us wear masks at some time or other. Part of mask wearing is necessary. Why go around letting people know exactly how we feel? If I have a splitting headache, I don't have to advertise it. If I'm feeling physically run-down, who wants to hear all the details? When we're troubled we don't mind sharing with a few close friends, but we don't tell the whole world that we're struggling.

Real lovers, however, learn to unmask themselves and allow the other to do the same. They strive for honesty and to get beyond wearing masks in each other's presence.

When couples first date, they are on their best behavior. They want to be liked. They tend to follow the style of behavior that they think the other one expects. Some folks never take off the mask. They think the other may want a comic, and so they've always got a clever joke rather than allowing serious conversation. Some men have to be Mr. Macho, always talking in manly language and showing aggressive behavior.

Some women put on the mask of the seductress. Others wear the poor-little-me mask. There are all kinds of masks that people wear, but true lovers work at getting beyond the surface. They want to understand and to be understood.

I remember when I was in seminary, there was a female student whom I considered aloof and unsocial. One day in chapel she sat next to me, simply because it was the first place available. It was an informal service that day, and the speaker talked about sharing ourselves. He included instructions that went something like this: "Turn to the person sitting next to you. Share one feeling you have about yourself. Take a risk and do it."

The young lady turned to me and said, "I'm scared. I don't know if I'm going to make it in seminary."

She said other things, but for the first time she had taken off her mask in my presence. I saw, beneath the public image, a frightened young woman. And because she expressed her fear to me, I felt compassion and understanding.

That's the way real love works. The more we open ourselves to each other, the more we understand each other, and the more we understand each other, the more honest we are with ourselves and with God.

True lovers work lovingly at unmasking each other.

All-seeing God, help _____ and me to unmask ourselves before each other, that we might love each other better as we love you together. Amen.

HONEST LOVE

[Jesus said,] "… whatever is in your heart determines what you say." (Matthew 12:34)

Week 4, Day 5

Often the words we say reflect not only what we think, but also the deeper feelings that are inside. Jesus said, "The mouth speaks what the heart is full of." Each word we say carries with it a certain feeling or vibration which can be destructive or uplifting. We make those kinds of choices.

We can understand a great deal about the character of another person by listening to the words he or she uses. Our words betray us more than we realize.

When Jesus was being tried by Pilate and Peter denied knowing him, a little maiden insisted that he was one of Jesus' followers. Bystanders said, "Your accent betrays you." They meant, of course, that his accent or his phraseology told that he was from the same part of the country that Jesus was.

Our speech betrays all of us. If we are truly loving and sensitive people, our words will portray that. No matter how hard we try, if we're cold, indifferent, or harsh, somehow this comes out through our words.

Good lovers learn to be honest with each other. They learn to deal honestly with their feelings and with their attitudes. They take the risk of saying how they feel, knowing that the other is going to respond with acceptance.

Before we can be fully honest with each other, we first have to learn to be honest with ourselves. We face up to how we think and feel about events, people, and things in our world.

Honesty between lovers means letting the other know what we feel, but doing it in a way that does not purposely hurt the other person. Real lovers seek the kind of intimacy that says, "I can tell you any of my deep thoughts, and I know you will understand."

God, teach us to be honest with each other as we try to be honest with you. Amen.

THANKFUL LOVERS

Be thankful in all circumstances, for this is God's will for you who belong to Christ Jesus. (1 Thessalonians 5:18)

Week 4, Day 6

This morning I was praying before going to work. One of the first things I did was to thank God for Shirley. I took a few minutes telling God how wonderful she was and how thankful I was to be her husband. Shirley wasn't feeling well, and I prayed for her physical health. I gave thanks to God that he had seen fit to give me such a wonderful wife.

Of all the great lessons I've learned in life, particularly since I've been a Christian, one of the most helpful has been learning to give thanks. I've tried over the years to be aware of the good things that happen in my life and to thank God for them. When I pray I often spend much of the prayer time thanking God for special people: for Shirley, for my children, for good friends.

In recent years I've been able to look back and thank God for what seemed, at the time, to be tragedies. Some of those hardships brought me to where

I am today. I can look back and I can think of two or three girls that I might have married. I'm thankful now that I didn't. God gave me a wife fitted for my needs, just as he did for Adam. (See Genesis 2:18). I can think back on career opportunities that I turned down. I'm glad I did. At the time I wasn't sure, but in reflection I know I made the right decisions.

A few years ago in my devotional reading I came across 1 Thessalonians 5:18, and it struck me as though I had never read it before. Paul exhorts us to give thanks in every situation, though he's not saying to give thanks for every circumstance. Because we are God's people, in the midst of all of our trials and no matter how bad things appear, we can give thanks to God.

Yesterday afternoon a young couple came to see me. For thirty-five minutes they told me all their problems. He had lost his job, they had no money to pay their rent, and there was practically no food in the house. Everything was going wrong. They recited one problem after another. When they finally finished, they looked at each other as Mike took his wife's hand and said, "The one thing I've got to be thankful for is that my wife has stood with me."

Out of the midst of all those horrible circumstances beamed one bright ray of sunshine: their faces showed that they loved each other. Mike knew his problems weren't going to be solved immediately, but they both knew they had each other.

In the midst of the deepest possible troubles we can still give thanks that we have each other, because that's what makes the difference.

God of grace and power, we thank you for each other, just as together we thank you for you. Amen.

Loyal Lovers

Love never gives up, never loses faith, is always hopeful, and endures through every circumstance. (1 Corinthians 13:7)

Week 4, Day 7

Shirley was summarizing what a friend had said to her. "Jan began telling me how unmotivated her husband is, and that he has no serious goal in life. Then she said, 'And, honestly, I don't know how you put up with Cec. He's brusque and—'"

"Wait a minute," Shirley interrupted, and I could picture those blue eyes blazing. "Cec is my husband. I love him, and I won't have you speaking against him in my presence."

Jan had attempted to tear me down, and Shirley's loving loyalty wouldn't allow that.

Loyalty doesn't mean closing one's eyes and ignoring reality. It doesn't mean denying truth. But loyalty says, "I love him/her. I will not speak against or belittle my love."

We belittle so easily. "My wife couldn't boil water when we met. Now she overboils it." "My husband thought that the receptacle for dirty clothes was the middle of the bedroom floor."

Soon others join in. I have too strong a sense of loyalty to Shirley to participate, and she likewise. If she has defects, you'll not know it from me.

Father-friend, always make me loyal to _____, and help me to never belittle or speak against him/her. Amen.

KEEPING SCORE

[Love] … does not demand its own way. It is not irritable, and it keeps no record of being wronged. (1 Corinthians 13:5)

Week 5, Day 1

For a few months in my junior year of high school, I dated Jean. I also worked after school and often ran into a time problem of picking her up, going out for a date, and getting her home at a reasonable hour. When I worked overtime, I'd ask her to meet me near where I worked.

One evening I called and asked her to meet me. "No," she said, "I've done this eight times before, and I'm not going to do it again." She didn't. We never dated after that, either.

I laugh now at Jean keeping score. But a lot of people do. They remember every slight, every misspoken word, every mistake. They can tell you exactly how many times you've done anything wrong.

True love doesn't hold on to mistakes. True love forgives and forgets. Forgetting means it's as though it never happened. God's love treats us that way.

When we confess sin, he forgives and doesn't bring it up again.

True lovers treat each other that way. They forgive and forgive and forgive. They forgive without even being asked. "Love… will hardly even notice when others do it wrong."

Some people have trouble forgiving and not holding grudges. I suspect they have trouble also in believing they've been forgiven. Because they haven't experienced forgiving love, it's hard for them to give it. Real lovers help each other learn to forgive by forgiving first. They teach by the way they live that we can bury the mistakes of the past.

A few months ago, a couple who had been married nearly twenty years related an experience from their courtship days. "We had a terrible row," he said. "We yelled at each other and I stormed off." He paused and looked at his wife. "Honey, do you remember what we argued about?"

She thought for a minute and said, "No, I don't. I only remember that when you walked away, I ran after you and that ended it."

Love never keeps score and always forgets the bad.

Lord God, help me remember the good, forget the bad, and be quick to forgive. Amen.

KIND LOVE

Once we were safe on shore, we learned that we were on the island of Malta. The people of the island were very kind to us. It was cold and rainy, so they built a fire on the shore to welcome us. (Acts 28:1–2)

Week 5, Day 2

Shirley and I developed a custom in the early days of our dating. We made each other cards on special occasions. The first valentine she gave me was a hand-drawn card, and she's no artist. That's the way we've done it through the years. Homemade cards for birthdays, anniversaries, and special occasions.

When I taught school and brown-bagged it, Shirley used to pack my sandwiches. Somewhere in the bag I'd find a little note that said, "I love you."

We've used that method over the years as one of our little ways of saying to each other, "I love you and I won't forget you."

Those little acts of kindness we do for each other build a stronger relationship. We don't want to take each other for granted, even though we have assurance of the other's love.

True love is always looking for ways of being helpful and considerate. Love always wants to make life better and more enjoyable for the other.

We all grow through kindness extended to us by other people.

In Acts 28, Paul, Luke, and others, after surviving a shipwreck, landed at Malta. Luke wrote that the natives showed them remarkable kindness.

Kindness meant then, as it always does, action beyond the expected. It surpasses the conventional or the required.

True lovers constantly look for ways to express their love for each other. They want fresh approaches to communicate the message "I love you; you're important to me."

God of kindness, you constantly give us more than we expect or deserve. Help us find ways of showing our love and commitment to each other. Amen.

UNCONDITIONAL LOVE

Be kind to each other, tenderhearted, forgiving one another, just as God through Christ has forgiven you. (Ephesians 4:32)

Week 5, Day 3

A couple came to me about a year ago and asked me to perform their marriage. As we began to talk, the woman handed me a piece of paper. She said, "This is the vow we want to make to each other." The long paragraph of promises concluded with "as long as we both shall love."

As we talked further, I began to realize she had put conditions on her love. Without actually saying it in words, she communicated that she would love her husband as long as he did things that she believed he ought to do. She was saying, "As long as you operate by my rules, I will love you. When you stop using those rules, I will stop loving you."

True love doesn't work that way. True love is absolutely unconditional. Unconditional love means I accept you for who you are, for all your strengths and your weaknesses.

The verse that is often called the gospel in a nut-shell, John 3:16, begins, "For God so loved the world …" God gave that statement of unconditional love. He loved, and he gave. We don't have to be good; we don't have to reach a certain level of attainment. God doesn't love us as long as we're good or as long as we behave. His love never ends. When two people love each other, but put conditions on it, they really say, "I expect you to live up to my arbitrary stand-ards, and I will live up to your expectations. If either of us comes up short, our love will dissolve." That's a no-win game, because nobody ever fully lives up to anyone else's expectations.

On the other hand, I remember an example of unconditional love. A year after Shirley and I mar-ried, we joined a church. Don belonged to the same church, and I didn't like him. I found him irritat-ing and difficult to get along with. Yet every time I turned around, Don seemed to be there. He would even come to see me. We had a lot of ups and downs in our relationship, but eventually I learned to like him.

He once said to me, "I chose you to be my friend. I love you as a friend. My love for you was not condi-tioned upon your response."

I'm not sure that most of us can love someone and accept that person whether or not it's recipro-cated. But that's what real love is. It's to love whether or not we're loved in return. That's the kind of love that God pours out to us. It's also mature love, the kind that we want as lovers to offer each other. This love has no strings attached, and no conditions. We say "I love you." Period.

God, you put no conditions upon your love to us. Help us to love each other without strings attached. Amen.

"I LOVE YOU, BUT…"

[Jesus said,] "Those the Father has given me will come to me, and I will never reject them. (John 6:37)

Week 5, Day 4

Ever say to a person, "I love you, but…"?

A sentence beginning with but, as I remember from high school English, implies a statement of contrast, and usually of rebuttal. Often the but begins the real meaning. Any prior words act only to set the person up for what we really want to say.

"You have so much talent, but…"

"You are beautiful, but…"

"You have a brilliant mind, but…"

Let's avoid those statements. Especially let's learn not to say them to the person we love and plan to spend the rest of our lives with.

When we have to add anything besides a period to "I love you," we need to check ourselves out, and our feelings!

When I have to add words, I am discounting, judging, belittling, or perhaps simply not accepting. "I love you, but your nose is too long" or "your teeth are crooked." Those words communicate nonacceptance. They imply rejection.

Lovers know the object of affection isn't perfect, but they accept imperfection as part of that individual. They love the other. Period.

This became clear to me a few years ago when, with a dozen couples, Shirley and I played a game at a church social. Each of us who didn't know the game went into a room one at a time. I was asked, "What does Shirley consider your worst fault?"

I answered, "She doesn't think I have any." They laughed.

When Shirley came in, they asked, "What's Cec's worst fault?"

Without a hint of hesitation she said, "He doesn't have any." This time they didn't laugh.

What they didn't understand was that Shirley and I accept each other as we are, not for what we can make the other into, not for the potential we see. We love the person who now is.

I know that's right for lovers because it's the way God views us. Jesus made that clear when he said, "No one who comes to me will I reject." God's love accepts us as we are (cf Romans 5:8). He saves us simply because he loves us as we are. God never adds but when he tells us about his love for us. I believe in following that example.

Heavenly Father, I love _____. Help me accept the way he/she is, in the same way you accept me without any qualifying statements. Amen.

Love that Lasts

I pray that your love will overflow more and more, and that you will keep on growing in knowledge and understanding. (Philippians 1:9)

Week 5, Day 5

I lectured at a local high school on love, romance, and sex. I followed this by a question-and-answer period.

One curly-haired fellow raised his hand and said, "I really love this girl, but how long will our love last?"

Several around him snickered, but I thought he asked a good question. I replied, "As long as you keep growing together."

A significant quality of true love relationships involves mutual growth. I am not the kind of lover today that I was yesterday or even a week ago. If my love is healthy and maturing, Shirley and I grow closer together; we are both becoming better people and stronger Christians.

When couples come to me for premarital counseling, one thing I urge is, "Find activities in which you both can be involved." A local congregation is one of the best places where Christian couples can become friends of the same group of people. Other ways to keep growing include common hobbies and common forms of recreation.

I think of other ways for lovers to grow. One of them is to affirm each other. I don't intend this as a gimmick, because I think appreciating and complimenting come naturally if we think about it. Every time I write an article for publication, Shirley reads over my shoulder and makes final suggestions before the last typing of the manuscript. The other day she was reading through the first part of this book of devotions. When she finished one she smiled, closed her eyes, and said, "Cec, that was beautiful." She affirmed me. By her affirmation of me I believe we both grew.

The young man in high school asked how long a love would survive. The Apostle Paul answered that question in 1 Corinthians 13 when he wrote that love never ends.

The final thing I want to say here about growing in love is that we grow as we spend time together with God. It isn't just going to church together. There's a special quality that emerges between couples who pray together, read the Bible together, and search for a closer walk with Jesus Christ together.

God of all the earth, help the two of us to grow together. And may our love never end, just as we know that our love for you will only get better. Amen.

GUILT

Then Jesus said to the woman, "Your sins are forgiven."
The men at the table said among themselves, "Who is this
man, that he goes around forgiving sins?" And Jesus said
to the woman, "Your faith has saved you, go in peace."
(Luke 7:48–50)

Week 5, Day 6

I dated Delores only three or four times. We first met when we were in the navy. We both worked in the legal department. She was beautiful, bright, and articulate—the kind of woman who appealed to me.

After the third or fourth date I didn't want to go out with her anymore. It took me a long time to figure out why. I finally realized that Delores made me feel guilty. She had a way of controlling me that I resented. She would use words like "you must…," "you ought to…," "you should…."

People often use guilt to control others. Mothers do this to their children, reminding them that they have given up so much for them. Children use it with their parents, saying in effect, "If you really love me, then you would do this for me." That produces guilt, and nobody wants to feel guilty. True lovers never induce guilt. In fact, real lovers alleviate guilt every opportunity they have.

Real lovers try to make the other person free— free to express the inner self, free to forget the past, free to move into the future. As two people become more intimate, they learn the hurting places of the other. One of the ways that they alleviate guilt is to say, "I understand."

There's a very poignant story in Luke's Gospel. A woman, obviously a prostitute, came to Jesus at the home of Simon, a Pharisee. Custom in those days required the host to have a servant who washed the guest of honor's feet. They denied Jesus this privilege and were in effect shunning him. This woman of the street came to the banquet, knelt by Jesus, and washed and dried his feet. Jesus recognized her devotion. He said, "You are forgiven. Go in peace."

The Pharisees were horrified that Jesus could say such things. He had relieved the woman's guilt, and she was free. He also said to those Pharisees, "I tell you, her sins—and they are many—have been forgiven, so she has shown me much love. But a person who is forgiven little shows only little love." (Luke 7:47)

True love wipes out guilt and wants the other to be totally free.

Lord God, help my lover and me to overcome guilt and to realize the freedom we have in Jesus Christ. Amen.

LOVING ME

We love each other because he loved us first. (1 John 4:19)

Week 5, Day 7

I had lunch with Frank the other day. In the course of our conversation he said, "I got knocked around a lot when I was a kid. I stayed a lot with relatives and grandparents, hardly ever with my own parents. I didn't think anybody loved me."

Frank had just gone through a divorce. He's already dating someone else, and at this stage I don't see much hope for success in this new relationship.

Frank admitted that he'd never felt loved by anyone in his life. That's the real key to loving relationships with other people. We have to know we're loved before we can love in return.

The Apostle John put it this way: We love (or are able to love) because God loved us first. This happens not only on the divine level, but the human as well. Children who are not loved do not know how to love. People who have received affection and attention know what it is like to receive it, and thereby learn to give it.

Sometimes we think that people are "stuck on themselves," self-conceited, or vain. We call them braggarts. Often these are the people who not only need to be loved the most, but don't love themselves and are constantly reaching for love.

True lovers know that they have to love themselves first before they can genuinely give themselves to the other. Self-love is healthy and normal. Loving myself is not selfish or self-centered. The more we know we are loved and the more we have received love, the more we tend to get away from self-centeredness.

When we genuinely love ourselves, we can fall in love with another human being; we want to do things for that person. Part of our love says, "Let me meet your needs." People who don't love themselves have unhealthy attitudes in relationships. Inwardly they're constantly crying, "Please love me. Please make me know that you care. Please assure me that I'm a worthwhile person."

The central message of the Bible is that God sees us as people whom he loves. We can love because he loved us first. We can establish good relationships with another individual because we know we are loved for ourselves.

God who created us, enable me to love myself in a healthy manner so that I can both receive love and give it. Amen.

SEPARATION

Teach these new disciples to obey all the commands I have given you. And be sure of this: I am with you always, even to the end of the age." (Matthew 28:20)

Week 6, Day 1

Shirley left seven days ago. She won't return until late tomorrow. And I miss her.

Separation always plays a difficult role for lovers. They miss each other's company. They miss the physical presence of the other. They miss the opportunity to share the deep and reflective moments that pass on, forgotten because they weren't shared.

For all the pain of separation, it has its values as well. It gives each of the lovers space to reflect on the relationship. It helps them put the other into proper perspective in life.

As Shirley's absence has gone on each day, I think of dozens of ways in which I appreciate her. She's an encourager to me when self-doubt strikes me. She knows how to look me in the eye and say, "Cec, I think you're wrong." Shirley has made my world wider and brighter by being part of me. She's helped me grow and stretch myself. I know that no matter which direction life takes me, I can count on her support.

She'll be back tomorrow, and I'll tell her a few of those things. Not that I have to tell her—she already knows. But it's important to me to say the words, and important to her to hear them. Somewhere between my speaking and her hearing, our love will be strengthened. We haven't wanted the separation, but it was one of those inevitable things that often happen to lovers (her job took her away).

Separations happen. Maybe we need them. Sometimes we become too dependent on the other and need to develop our own personhood.

I suspect that was one of the many reasons Jesus left his disciples after the resurrection. They had to stand on their own. The first disciples needed to grow as leaders themselves.

When Jesus left, according to Matthew's Gospel, his last words were a promise: "I am with you always." He promised his presence with them. In body, he is separated from us; but in his spirit, he is here.

Lord, whenever my love and I have to be separated, keep the presence of the other strong, even as we pray for an increased awareness of your presence with both of us. Amen.

BALANCE

Two people are better off than one, for they can help each other succeed. If one person falls, the other can reach out and help. But someone who falls alone is in real trouble. Likewise, two people lying close together can keep each other warm. But how can one be warm alone? A person standing alone can be attacked and defeated, but two can stand back-to-back and conquer. Three are even better, for a triple-braided cord is not easily broken. (Ecclesiastes 4:9–12)

Week 6, Day 2

A few years ago someone asked me, "What's the best thing Shirley does for you?"

After thinking for a few seconds I replied, "She gives me balance."

The inquirer had in mind something more of a domestic nature (cooking, cleaning, or mending), but I believe my answer is still right.

By nature, I'm compulsive, quick, energetic, and decisive. Shirley reacts deliberately, slowly, and analytically. Together our natures blend into a fuller, rounder person.

When two people meet and love each other, one balances the other. He supplies qualities she lacks. She supplements his inadequacies.

When the Preacher talks in Ecclesiastes about two being better than one, he is saying this also. One lifts the other during moments of weakness. She rubs his shoulder while he fights discouragement.

True lovers have an intuitive way of knowing how to provide the balance for each other. Strength balances weakness; health lifts up sickness. All of life works this way with lovers. Artists and photographers know that a good picture needs both light and shadow. Writers understand that good novels need both a protagonist and an antagonist. They contrast, but the contrast produces the balance.

As I've thought of Shirley and our relationship over the years, I often thank God for the balance she brings me and the harmony we share together.

Loving Lord, help us always balance each other, and in our harmony may we serve you together. Amen.

Decision Making

The Lord says, "I will guide you along the best pathway for your life. I will advise you and watch over you." (Psalm 32:8)

Week 6, Day 3

Lovers need to learn to make decisions: decisions that affect themselves personally and decisions that have to do with the whole relationship.

We influence—or even force—the other person to make decisions. Some people are quick-thinking and can come up with a dozen solutions to a problem. I tend to be that way. Others are the slower, plodding type, who think a problem through, analyze it carefully, and come up with a single solution. Sometimes we fast-talking types put the slower-thinking ones into a bind. We give them two or three options as though they have to choose between just those. In reality, they may have a totally different option which is much better.

A lot of decisions are made by default. One person finally throws up his hands and says, "Do anything you want; let's just do something." The slow person says, "Because you rushed me, you made me come to a decision that I wasn't ready to make. I didn't have time to think it through."

Unwittingly, lovers sometimes play that game with each other. Good decision making comes about because of several factors. I am a decisive kind of person. I see a problem, make an instant decision, and am ready to move on. Shirley tends to be the other way. She wants to think about it, ponder it, and then decide. We have both learned to talk it over, so that now I no longer rush her and she speeds up a little to my pace.

When couples make decisions together, one of them may be caught up in the agony of sorting out options, while the other can back off emotionally and bring a certain amount of objectivity to the situation. Good decision making between lovers does not come about because one has an idea and forces the other. Good decisions come because both of them state their feelings and preferences plainly, pray about it together, and sense the direction God wants them to take.

It doesn't matter how the decision is arrived at. Good lovers make the decisions together. Most of all, they learn that Jesus Christ helps them sort out the options.

Good decision making between lovers does not divide them, but leaves both of them feeling, "This is right." It actually strengthens the bond between them.

Almighty God, help us to make our decisions together as we seek guidance from you. Amen.

COMMON GOALS

Seek the Kingdom of God above all else, and live right-eously, and he will give you everything you need. (Matthew 6:33)

Week 6, Day 4

I remember a young couple who came to me for premarriage counseling. They had no common goal. She was nineteen, starry-eyes, and all she wanted was a husband and a houseful of babies. He, on the other hand, had ambitions that required lengthy education. He knew that in order for him to fulfill his aim it would mean putting off a family for at least six years. Even though both of them heard what the other said, neither accepted the other's goal. I urged them to give more serious considera-tion toward common goals before entering into marriage. They left that day, and I never heard from them again. I don't know if they married or resolved the situation.

I am convinced that if they married without arriv-ing at common goals, their life together was miser-able. She had no commitment toward his projected goals. Her father was a semiskilled laborer, and as far as she was concerned that was good enough for any man. After all, her father had provided adequately, if not bountifully, for the family. The man, on the other hand, came from an impoverished family and felt the need to forego immediate financial rewards in order to get the kind of job and pay that he wanted later on in life.

Lovers sometimes come to cross-points at the matter of common goals, and one reason is that they get their priorities wrong. Jesus preached what is called the Sermon on the Mount. The main lesson he gave on life is summed up in Matthew 6:33, "Seek the Kingdom of God above all else, and live righteously, and he will give you everything you need." That verse reminds us that when we establish God as number one in our lives and both seek God's will, we arrive at common goals. When we have common goals, with God's will first, we can live and work together in harmony.

Dear Lord, may our goals be the same, but may our highest goal be to love and serve you. Amen.

Making Allowances

Always be humble and gentle. Be patient with each other, making allowance for each other's faults because of your love. (Ephesians 4:2)

Week 6, Day 5

In a church meeting a few years ago Edna said some terrible things about me personally, which had to do with my leadership and my ineffectiveness. Her words were passionate and unrestrained. After the meeting she and I stood and had a cup of coffee together, and I put my arm around her. Later someone who had observed that said to me, "How could you do that after the way Edna talked about you?"

I'd known Edna for some time and loved her. I knew her well enough to know that she made angry statements, but once she said them she forgot them. I knew also that she was feeling contrite about what she had said. Edna had always been that way. I did not take her angry words personally. Because I knew her, I could make allowances. I loved her.

One of the marks of true relationships is the ability to make allowances for each other's faults. And we all have faults.

The wife may wake up slowly in the morning and talk with a snarl until 11:00. The husband abounds with energy early in the morning and hurries through the day, but by 8:00 at night he's dragging and easily irritated. True love makes allowances for differing temperaments.

True love never demands that the other become a carbon copy. We have differences. We learn to live with those differences and enjoy each other. I could think of nothing more boring than being married to a wife who was exactly like me. We would probably drive each other insane by being in continuous motion.

Lovers need to stop from time to time and ask themselves if they are making allowances for each other's differences. Must my loved one always conform to my image and my rules? Can we allow each other to be less than perfect? Different? Slower or faster? Mature love not only allows those differences; it accepts them. In our marriage, Shirley's differences and mine help make our marriage more exciting and stronger.

God of all, teach us to overlook each other's faults, knowing our faults are also overlooked. But most of all, increase our love to each other as it increases toward you. Amen.

Handling the Past

But God showed his great love for us by sending Christ to die for us while we were still sinners. (Romans 5:8)

Week 6, Day 6

The boys in the neighborhood knew all about Ruthie. At the age when we discovered sex and still had not moved beyond a whispering knowledge, Ruthie was miles ahead of us.

I didn't see Ruthie after tenth grade, until three years after I graduated from high school. I saw her sitting alone in a restaurant and asked if I could sit with her. She hesitated only a moment and then said, "Of course."

Almost immediately we caught up on the intervening years. Ruthie told me she was now married to Greg. In quick sentences she told me about this mechanic who fixed her car and asked her for a date. When Greg took her out, he didn't even try to kiss her. They went out three times before he ever held her hand.

"And you know why?" Ruthie said. "He said he loved me for who I was now." Apparently Greg had heard the stories of her past, but it didn't matter.

In one way or another we all have a past—the kind of things we've done but wouldn't want the world to know. For some, it may be a promiscuous period in life because of the need to be loved. For others, it might have been cheating on tests or pilfering from a store. Whatever our mistakes, we don't want them whispered or known.

Yet when real love comes along, our past doesn't make any difference. We are loved for who we are now. Real love doesn't reject us because of sins or mistakes of the past. We're accepted now.

When we love a person unreservedly, we imitate God's example of love for us. Paul, the greatest writer of the Bible, said that God proved his love for us in that while we were still sinners, he sent Christ to die for us.

I had become a Christian a few months before meeting Ruthie again. While we didn't talk about religion or Christ, I recognized that she had received the kind of love all of us need—the unconditional love of another.

"My past doesn't make any difference to him," she said. "And you know, it makes me want to be the kind of wife he wants. There just isn't anything I wouldn't do for Greg. He loves me for who I am."

That's love.

God, because you love both of us without any attached conditions, help us understand that love, and give it to each other. Amen.

DOUBT

But if you have doubts about whether If you do anything you believe is not right, you are sinning. (Romans 14:23)

Week 6, Day 7

Eleanor had graduated at the top of her college class. Talented, bright, witty, and lovely, she had more dates than she could handle. During her senior year, she thought about marriage. She looked at all the prospects and settled on Randy.

He had all the qualities she decided a husband ought to have. He was handsome, highly intelligent, athletic, and congenial. She responded to his invitation, and after graduation they married. Three years later they divorced.

She later admitted, "I ignored my inner feelings. Everyone kept telling me that we'd be happy and I wanted to believe them."

"Did you ever have doubts?" I asked her.

"They were there. I just wouldn't face them."

True lovers often go through periods of uncertainty. They wonder if they love enough. Will their love last? Will she be the right kind of partner? Can he live up to her expectations?

Doubts are normal. But to ignore the doubts—that's asking for trouble.

Saint Paul deals with doubt in Romans 14 when he writes about meat offered to idols. After removal from pagan temples, people could buy the meat at cut-rate prices. Some did and considered it a bargain. Others said it was worshiping demons (1 Corinthians 8). Paul simply says, "Do whatever you feel right about yourself. But don't stir up trouble. If you doubt, don't buy. If you have no problem over it, then it's okay."

Then he adds the clincher, "...whatever does not proceed from faith is sin" (Romans 14:23).

That applies to lovers, too. When I move toward marriage but reservations are still there, I am proceeding with doubt. And for me, as a child of God, that's wrong.

What's the answer? Wait. Pray. Talk together. Share your uneasiness. Don't get caught like Eleanor and Randy. Don't let your friends tell you that you're perfect for each other.

When two Christians who date want God's will for their lives, God will direct them. They can proceed on the basis of faith. But until that gut level assurance comes, don't.

Holy Spirit, if we're meant for each other, remove my doubts. If you have other plans for our lives, show us both. Amen.

HELPFUL HINTS FOR
MAKING LOVE LAST

1. The most beautiful words your lover can hear from you: "I love you." Say them often, at least once a day.

2. Praying lovers make better lovers. Jesus Christ becomes the special ingredient that cements the relationship and holds it together.

3. Be considerate. Continually do little things that show consideration, thoughtfulness, and kindness.

4. Allow each other privacy. Togetherness is important; sharing builds relationships. Private space gives both of you time to reflect and stretch.

5. Nobody's perfect—not even lovers. Don't tell the world about each other's imperfections. The best lovers have an intense loyalty to each other. They keep each other's secret faults secret.

6. Love is a relationship of trust, mutual respect, and acceptance. Love each other by your commitment and feelings.

7. It's not so much that opposites attract as that one complements the other. Together the two of you can become one complete person. That's the way God planned it.

8. Learn to listen. Don't just hear, but listen with your ears and eyes, and work at developing that kind of sense that detects needs in the other.

9. Lovers forgive. Remind yourself that you're human, vulnerable, and could just as easily have hurt the other. The more you're in touch with your feelings, the more easily you can pray, "Forgive us our trespasses, as we forgive those who trespass against us."

10. We all wear masks at times. As a lover, make yourself vulnerable. Remove your masks because you're developing and learning trust.

11. Don't compete, but rejoice at the good happenings in his/her life.

12. Don't put conditions upon your commitment, because love gives of itself and demands nothing in return, not even appreciation, acceptance, or obligation.

13. Thank God for each other. He/she is the most important person in your life. He/she is God's gift.

14. You can only love another person as you love yourself first. As you appreciate your own value, talents, and worth to God and others, you can also appreciate and love others and

establish that special relationship with him/her.

15. Speak honestly. The words may hurt, but you need to say them to express yourself. You also reveal the things you feel most deeply about.

16. Learn to share yourself. The more you open yourself, the more your lover can know the real you. The more you tell him/her about yourself, the more you also know yourself.

17. The more you have in common, the more you grow together in your relationship. You share the same friends, the same church, the same recreation and hobbies. Most of all, you share the same faith in Jesus Christ.

18. Don't try to possess your lover. Allow him/her to have friends—of both sexes. Build the relationship on trust where suspicion has no place.

19. Make decisions together. Discover each other's desires and biases. Then decide—together. That process itself strengthens the love relationship.

More Helpful Hints for Making Love Last

1. True lovers accommodate the one another. Some people don't like that statement, but real love says, "My spouse is as important as I am. I'll do what I can for her/him and she/he will do the same for me."
2. Lasting and happy marriages are built on a covenant. That covenant—a unity with each other under God—sustains the relationship and is more important then temporary emotions.
3. Your spouse's role in life is not to make you happy; your responsibility is not to make your spouse happy. Good marriages center on choosing to defer to the other's needs and desires.
4. Good manners toward your spouse do a great deal to keep a marriage happy. If men treat their wives the way they did during the dating period, and she does the same for him, such behavior goes a long way toward sustaining a loving relationship.

5. The best principle I know about marriage is simple: Treat your mate the way you want to be treated. We build a relationship not on receiving love, but on giving it. We give it by offering ourselves to each other.

DEVOTIONS FOR DIETERS

IGNORANCE PAYS

Regarding your question about the special abilities the Spirit gives us. I don't want you to misunderstand this. (1 Corinthians 12:1)

In my mid-thirties I became aware of my increased weight. "I'll have to do something about it," I said to myself and my wife several times.

Then I took the plunge and started out. Over the years I had accumulated incorrect information such as: proteins help you lose weight and carbohydrates make you gain. For the next week I loaded up on protein—eating meat almost exclusively, and lots of it. I particularly liked salami, polish sausage, and pork chops. Somehow that idea didn't work. I actually put on two pounds.

I tried cutting out desserts and eliminating sugar and milk in my coffee. However, a little marmalade on my toast didn't count much. Ice milk wasn't as fattening as ice cream. I kept gaining.

It took a few more years and frustrated dieting before I realized a stark truth: ignorance pays the wrong kind of dividends.

Like a lot of people who wanted to drop off the pounds, I went about it the wrong way. It was only when I learned about nutrition and sensible calorie counting that the excess baggage started disappearing.

The Apostle Paul understood about ignorance. He wrote to the Corinthian church about that very subject. They had been a greatly blessed church—he said in the first chapter that they lacked nothing in spiritual gifts. But the apostle had a lot of straightening out to do with that local congregation. In chapters 12–14 he wrote about the meaning, purpose, and use of these gifts. But he prefaced his remarks with these words: "Now concerning spiritual gifts, brethren, I do not want you to be uninformed."

Because they had been ignorant, they had all kinds of confusion in that congregation. He wrote to enlighten them and set them straight.

Knowing we need to lose weight, plus a few isolated facts, aren't enough. We need to learn about nutrition. We need to learn how our body operates. As we learn more, we not only rid ourselves of misinformation, but we learn how to slim down and live with a body that's healthier and happier.

Great Teacher, help me learn about calories and losing weight. Don't let me foolishly do all the wrong things in a misguided attempt to drop off pounds. Amen.

Facing Myself

But don't just listen to God's word. You must do what it says. Otherwise, you are only fooling yourselves. For if you listen to the word and don't obey, it is like glancing at your face in a mirror. You see yourself, walk away, and forget what you look like. (James 1:22–24)

I'll never forget the day that I made my decision to count calories. I had come out of the shower, and standing in the bathroom I saw a side view of myself. I didn't like what I saw: a paunchy stomach, flabby arms, thickening thighs, a collar size a full inch bigger than it had ever been before in my life. That's when I decided to do something about it. And I did! I determined that day I would begin to count calories and would not stop until I had lost at least twenty-five pounds.

That may not sound like a lot of weight for some people to lose, but every pound is hard to lose. It meant not only a commitment to counting calories, a strict discipline, but it also entailed at least two other things.

First, I had to be honest with God and myself. I wanted to lose weight. I determined to become a trim person, even when old habits kept attacking me. I often prayed, "Lord, help me stick to my diet, even when I don't want to."

The other thing is, I knew I would fail once in a while. I had to learn to forgive myself. Forgiving myself meant saying to God and to Cec, "Okay, you blew it. Do better next time."

I learned that I couldn't just see that I needed to lose weight, I had to do something about it. By acting on my concern, I became the kind of person the Apostle James commends when he says it isn't enough to hear God's Word. We must also obey it. Those who only hear are like people who see themselves in a mirror and then forget what they look like. I had seen my flabby self many times and quickly erased the visual image. But the day I started to count calories I not only saw my image; I determined to change it. With God's help I have done that.

Lord Jesus, thank you for showing me myself. Help me to remember what I look like and give me a vision of what I can be. Amen.

SECRET SINS

You spread out our sins before you—our secret sins—and you see them all. (Psalm 90:8)

A health spa sign proclaimed, WHAT YOU EAT IN PRIVATE SHOWS UP IN PUBLIC. Next to the sign stood the scales. For me this graphically illustrates that we get away with nothing. Some people on diets seem to think that a tiny cookie, an extra spoonful of mashed potatoes and gravy, or only a small piece of cake won't count; no one will know. But we never really get away with anything. Still we keep trying to deceive others and ourselves.

Sometimes I've watched people eat forbidden food or extra amounts, discount it with a smile and say, "I'll have to run around the block a couple of extra times." I don't think they ever run around the block a couple of extra times. Even if they did, that wouldn't make up for the overindulgence.

We all get caught in the secret sin syndrome. Sometimes we think we can do something wrong— a sin which isn't very bad—and it won't count. Or later we can ask God to forgive us and no one will know. But no sin is ever secret, because God knows.

We need to remind ourselves that when we count calories we're not only helping our bodies; we're also trying to please God, and we don't please him by cheating.

Lord God, as a calorie counter help me to be honest with you and with myself, in public or in secret. Amen

About the Author

New York Times bestselling author Cecil (Cec) Murphey has written or co-written more than 135 books, including the bestsellers *90 Minutes in Heaven* (with Don Piper) and *Gifted Hands: The Ben Carson Story* (with Dr. Ben Carson). His books have sold in the millions and have brought hope and encouragement to countless people around the world.

Visit his website at www.CecilMurphey.com and follow him on Twitter at www.Twitter.com/CecMurphey.